M000006881

ALONG THE HIGH ROAD

ALONG THE HIGH ROAD

A Guide to the Scenic Route between Espanola and Taos

Text and Photography by
Margaret M. Nava

SUNSTONE
PRESS

SANTA FE

© 2004 by Margaret M. Nava. All rights reserved.

No part of this book may be reproduced in any form or by any electronic
or mechanical means including information storage and retrieval systems
without permission in writing from the publisher,
except by a reviewer who may quote brief passages in a review.

Sunstone books may be purchased for educational, business, or sales promotional use.
For information please write: Special Markets Department, Sunstone Press,
P.O. Box 2321, Santa Fe, New Mexico 87504-2321.

Library of Congress Cataloging-in-Publication Data

Nava, Margaret M.
    Along the high road : a guide to New Mexico's high road to Taos / text
and photography by Margaret M. Nava.
      p. cm.
    ISBN 0-86534-413-2 (pbk.)
    1. Taos Region (N.M.)—Tours. 2. Scenic byways—New Mexico—Taos
Region—Guidebooks. 3. Cities and towns—New Mexico—Taos
Region—Guidebooks. 4. Taos Region (N.M.)—History, Local. 5. Taos
Region (N.M.)—Social life and customs. I. Title.
F804.T2 N38 2004
917.89'5304—dc22

                            2003017930

Published in SUNSTONE PRESS
POST OFFICE BOX 2321
SANTA FE, NM 87504-2321 / USA
(505) 988-4418 / ORDERS ONLY (800) 243-5644
FAX (505) 988-1025
WWW.SUNSTONEPRESS.COM

To Dad

Sorry you never got to know the real New Mexico

CONTENTS

ACKNOWLEDGEMENTS

An author never writes alone. There are always people who read the manuscript, make suggestions, offer advice, or just give much needed support. I would like to thank all the people along the High Road who opened their homes to me, patiently answered my questions, and allowed me to take photographs. Also, to the New Mexico State Highway Department...thank you for all those wonderful Historic Markers. Not only were they informative, they added a much-needed dimension to this book. Of course, to my brother and his wife...thank you for your continuing love and support. I couldn't have done this without your encouragement.

PREFACE

As vacationers in New Mexico, my family and I often drove the road between Santa Fe and Taos, our two favorite places in the state. Confident that we were seeing the real New Mexico, we sped from one town to the next almost oblivious to what we were passing through. Sure, we fell in love with the countryside but once we reached our destination, we forgot the scenery and pursued more mundane activities. We shopped in elegant boutiques and galleries, drank strawberry margaritas, ate nouvelle cuisine, and stayed in sumptuous hotels. What were we thinking?

About a week after I finally made New Mexico my home, I took a ride, this time alone, down that same road. What I saw amazed me. There were old adobe homes lovingly cared for and surrounded by an array of flowers that would inspire any painter, chile ristras hanging from rooflines, and children playing peacefully in the yards. Outside some of the homes, artists hung placards advertising their professions: sculptor, weaver, painter, smith, or potter. And the churches – it seemed every town had its own. There was a feel about this place – one of peace, contentment, and cultural unity.

Since that early trip, I've made the drive several times. From beginning to end, it covers about fifty miles and passes through towns with names like Chimayo, Cordova, Truchas, and Las Trampas. If I observe the speed limit and don't make too many stops, I can complete the trip in about three hours although many people breeze through in less. They drive the serpentine roads, gaze at quaint houses and magnificent scenery, and come away convinced they have just taken a very scenic road trip. True, they've seen the valleys and mountains but what have they missed in between?

Some years back, M. Scott Peck wrote a book entitled The Road Less Traveled that advocated unconditional love, traditional values, and spiritual grown. His is a book about the difficulty and consequences of making choices in which Peck envisioned life as a road with each traveler choosing his or her own way – some taking the easy way, others the road less traveled. Every time I read Mr. Peck's book I think about New Mexico's High Road and the people that live there. They are people who – tied to the earth, fiercely independent, and tenaciously religious – settled a hostile land, created a new life for themselves, and became the moral fiber of New Mexico. They took the road less traveled. Are they out of step with the times or simply in tune with their environment? Take the drive along the High Road and decide for yourself.

Drive slowly through the villages. Talk to the people and hear their stories. Listen to the wind in the trees and the birds in the air. Smell the chiles and posole. Learn about the Santos and Santeros. Stay overnight in a secluded hacienda or serene farmhouse. But whatever you do, take your time. Only in that way will you come to know life as it was, and still is, along New Mexico's High Road to Taos.

—M. M. Nava
Rio Rancho, New Mexico, 2003

ABOUT THIS BOOK

A drive Along the High Road to Taos is more than a scenic road trip. It is a journey through the lives, values, and arts of the people who inhabit the small towns along the road. This book was written to familiarize you with those people in order that you might better understand and enjoy your experience. Each section of the book deserves special attention if you hope to truly perceive the essence of the people and their towns.

PART I

The Historic Background section of this book contains a simplified, often opinionated, early history of the region with descriptions of local art forms and the people who created them. It is short for a reason—living history is a better teacher than a book. This book will serve as a primer or introduction to what you will personally discover Along the High Road.

PART II

This section, divided into towns, provides specific historic information about each town (when it was founded, what happened there, etc.) as well as what to see, where to eat, and where to stay when you get there. The individual listings are alphabetic and have not been rated because each offers something unusual - each traveler should decide what suits him, or her, best. After the listings, space has been provided for travelers to record their experiences and observances.

Considering the limited amount of services available Along the High Road, it is a good idea to call ahead for reservations and/or hours of operation. These are small towns and sometimes the proprietors need time to care for farm animals or family matters.

Also, while visiting any establishment or locale, please be aware that these are very private people who may not welcome photography and/or curious tourists. ASK FIRST should be your standard approach.

Drive the roads slowly, observe posted limits, and be prepared to pull over to let locals pass.

PART III

The final section of this book contains lists of books and museums that will further your knowledge and enjoyment of the people, towns, values, and arts you will discover Along the High Road.

ENJOY THE JOURNEY

PART I

HISTORIC BACKGROUND

THE PAST

The three essentials for settling New Spain's Northern Frontier were soldiers, priests, and of course, settlers. Don Juan de Onate, a wealthy resident of Zacatecas, Mexico, had all three. In July of 1598, after several arduous months of traveling north along the Rio Grande, Onate and his league arrived at an area near an Indian pueblo they promptly named San Juan de los Cabelleros. Along the south side of the Santa Cruz River, the soldiers set up camp, Onate proclaimed himself governor, and the priests began the serious matter of converting the Indians. Within a couple of years, settlers established small ranches along both sides of the river at La Canada (the canyon). They raised cattle, horses, and with the help of the Indians, crops. But all was not well.

Throughout Spain's Northern Frontier, Indians were feeling the affects of colonization, and they didn't like it. They believed the colonists were taking over their ancestral lands, forcing a mysterious religion on them, and by and large abusing them. In August of 1680, the Pueblo people joined forces and rebelled. The Indians destroyed the colonists' crops, burned their churches, and occupied their homes. In the process, they also killed families, farmers, and priests. Colonists that survived escaped to the south. But this was not a total victory for the Pueblos; twelve years later, the colonists returned.

In 1692 Don Diego de Vargas Zapata Lujan Ponce de Leon, new governor for the territory, gathered his army outside the walls of Santa Fe and told the Pueblo Indians then living in Spanish-built houses that if they accepted each others' differences, shared the land, and complied with certain conditions, colonists and Indians could live together in peace. The Santa Fe Indians may not have been convinced but they were desperate and starving. Fighting had already broken out among the Pueblo villages and the Apache and Comanche were attacking. Before the Revolt, colonists helped by providing food and tools; now these supplies were hard to come by. The Indians in Santa Fe found themselves between a rock and a hard place so they reluctantly agreed to de Vargas' terms. It was four more years before the colonists took control of the other Pueblos, but ultimately, they once again dominated the Northern Frontier.

In the years following Spain's reentry into New Mexico after the Pueblo Revolt, Spanish colonists gradually resettled the Northern Frontier. Living in sparsely populated villages they raised families, tilled the soil, prayed to God for assistance, and distanced themselves from the governmental suppression and cultural turmoil that surrounded them.

As the population grew so too did the need for a land grant system. The first such grant, issued by de Vargas in 1695, established the new settlement of La Villa Nueva de Santa Cruz de los Espanoles Mejicanos del Rey Nuestro Senor Carlo Segundo. With its establishment, Santa Cruz became the second of three royal villas formally decreed by the Spanish Crown as military, administrative, and religious centers; the first was Santa Fe in 1692; the third was Albuquerque in 1706.

Romantics might have described the colonists' lifestyle as an idyllic existence in a pastoral setting but the isolation was a double-edged sword. Hostile Indian attacks, poor roads, and severe weather radically limited access to material goods forcing the settlers along New Spain's Northern Frontier to depend upon their own creativity to produce tools, clothing, and furnishings. The products of their creative talents, however, eventually set them apart from their Old World contemporaries.

SANTOS AND SANTEROS

Being mostly Catholic, the practice of religion played a crucial role in the colonists' lives. Although Franciscan friars established numerous missions during earlier expeditions to the area, the Pueblo Revolt left many churches destroyed or abandoned. Following the revolt, most of the friars, fearing for their lives, retreated to safer areas. The colonists were on their own. In order to preserve the core values of their faith, they built, or rebuilt, churches and devised unique religious customs based on, but deviating greatly from, Renaissance rituals.

The new churches, however, lacked the adornments essential in the process of conducting religious services. The colonists believed their services incomplete without these adornments and, therefore, created Santos (rustic carvings and paintings representing Christ, the Holy Family, saints, and angels) produced from local materials such as aspen, cottonwood, or tanned hides, and painted with water-soluble vegetable or mineral dyes.

There were two types of Santos. The two-dimension retalbos (panel paintings) were flat and most often rectangular in shape. The three-dimensional bultos (in the round) were carved figures. Both forms were made from seasoned wood coated with gypsum and glue (yeso or gesso) then painted and sealed. Sometimes clothed in garments either, or both, might appear in altar screens (Reredos) that had niches (nichos) built into the façade.

Although used primarily for devotion and prayer, the Santos played significant roles in the lives of the family or village to which they belonged. Each Santo fulfilled a special purpose; some were associated with the care of children while others granted favors, protected travelers, aided farmers, or provided relief from serious illness. Although any, and all, representations of the Cristo (Christ crucified) and the Virgen (Blessed Mother) elicited the highest esteem, San Juan (patron of sheep and shepherds), San Geronimo (protector against lightning), San Lorenzo (protector against fire), and San Ysidro (patron of farmers) were among the significant favorites. Obviously, in an agrarian society besieged by unpredictable and often extreme weather, any help was welcomed.

Santos became familiar figures in the Spanish settlements. Altars festooned with tiny silver Milagros (offerings of thanks for favors granted) and holding beloved Santos, appeared in most homes. The colonists considered the Santos members of their families and treated them like children, dressing them in clothing, setting meals out for them, rewarding them when they answered prayers, and punishing them when they did not. Considering the difficulty of the times, it is safe to assume that many a Santo found itself spending a great deal of time facing a wall.

The men who created the Santos were known as Santeros; the earliest were Franciscan friars who replicated Baroque or Mexican religious paintings and statues. Although the friars established fundamentals for producing the Santos, it was the lay clergy who, with little or no artistic training, perfected the art. While the work of the friars reflected a familiarization with architecture, anatomy, and perspective, that of later Santeros possessed a rural, unsophisticated quality. Today, each artist is easily identifiable because of his unique use of colors or unusual designs although, because of the frequency of unsigned work, many people believe the Santeros shied away from any recognition or appreciation for their holy accomplishments.

THE PENITENTES

Another group that resisted recognition was the brotherhood of La Fraternidad de los Hermanos de Nuestro Padre Jesus Nazareno, more simply known as Los Hermanos or the Penitentes. Although its exact origin is unknown, Los Hermanos formed to carry out obligations left unattended because of infrequent or rare visits by the clergy. Without priests and in an isolated area, it became the duty of the people to sustain themselves spiritually as well as materially, physically, and socially. The Penitentes fulfilled every aspect of that duty. As providers of the spiritual and temporal needs of the colonists, brotherhood members administered justice, supplied sustenance and support to widows and orphans, nursed the sick, buried the dead, and organized village feasts and religious ceremonies.

Membership in Los Hermanos, however, was not for everyone. Members, be they men (Penitentes) or later, women (Penitentas), devoted themselves to Christ and led exemplary Christian lives. This often meant giving up what little they owned and performing acts of penance to atone for their sins as well as those of others. It was a hard and exacting life that few could follow.

The Penitentes conducted many of their religious ceremonies in or around chapels known as moradas. The moradas were simple structures, typically without windows, very simply decorated: inside with candles and Santos and outside with a wooden cross. A carved skeletal figure of death, Dona Sebastiana, dressed in black and carrying a bow with arrow, was carried in procession to remind Penitente members of their mortality and the need to prepare for a good death. It's entirely possible Sebastiana was a precursor of things to come.

Word of Los Hermanos' unconventional activities reached church officials in Santa Fe and elicited immediate censure. The church's initial view was that the Penitentes, because of lack of adequate direction from clergy, were misguided and had to be brought back into the protective fold of the Roman Catholic Church. Toward that end, in 1833 Bishop Antonio Zubiria read a pastoral letter to the congregation at Santa Cruz forbidding membership in and demanding the immediate abolishment of the Penitente brotherhood. The remoteness of the northern villages and lack of sufficient clergy to carry out his wishes prevented enforcement of the orders and Zubiria's demands fell on deaf ears.

When Bishop Jean Baptiste Lamy arrived in Santa Fe in 1851, both the Penitentes and the Santos appalled him. From Lamy's puritanical European point of view, the colonists' religious practices were grotesque and idolatrous; neither were devout nor acceptable representations of the Catholic Faith. Blaming the Franciscan friars for the colonists' moral corruption, Lamy launched a personal campaign to discipline the priests and colonists and thereby regain control over New Mexico's Catholic provinces.

Reports that the Penitentes practiced extreme forms of self-discipline and penance led Lamy to insist that members put an end to their heretical practices and renounce their illicit membership before receiving the Holy Sacraments. Declaring the Santos profane parodies of religious art, he ordered them destroyed. Unknown to Lamy, the Penitentes continued their rituals in secrecy and hid their few remaining Santos.

After Lamy's retirement in 1885, Jean Baptiste Salpointe took up the struggle. Rather than just reproaching Los Hermanos members for their practices, Salpointe declared that the Penitentes originated from a former European group know as the Third

Order of St. Francis whose rules included leading a life of simplicity, humility, peacefulness, and piety. Even though Los Hermanos members fulfilled the first four requirements, their penitential practices were considered an unorthodox aberration of the Third Order and, as such, reflected unfavorably upon the Roman Catholic Church. If the brotherhood was to continue, its members had to abide by Church rules. Those who did not conform would be excommunicated. Salpointe's decree was a threat worse than death for most practicing Catholics but, it must be remembered, the Penitentes had been so long estranged from the Roman Catholic Church that they no longer felt the need to adhere to its rules.

If it is true that adversity builds strength, then by bonding together and holding fast their principles, the brotherhood grew stronger. Ceremonies and rituals continued as before but with even more security. Outsiders were not allowed and those who penetrated sacrosanct Penitente territory were dealt with harshly. It wasn't until 1947 that, by proclamation of Archbishop Edwin Vincent Byrne, Los Hermanos was finally recognized as an acceptable, although controversial, Catholic society of obscure origin and questionable philosophy.

In recent years, many secular writers have characterized the Penitentes as a notorious group of men who, shrouded in secrecy, carry out nefarious acts of self-penance. Such sensationalism ignores the good deeds and basic tenets that have been the cornerstones of the organization since its inception. In his book The Sacred World of the Penitentes, Alberto Lopez Pulido identifies these tenets as acts of "caridad (charity), oracion (prayer), and el buen ejemplo (the good example)"—hardly notorious but certainly worthy of praise.

THE WEAVERS

Francisco Vasquez de Coronado brought the first Churro sheep to North America in 1540. Two years later, when his search for gold and riches proved fruitless, Coronado retreated to Mexico and left the sheep behind. Despite the harsh climate, the sheep thrived and became an important part of the Spanish colonies' economy providing settlers with food and fiber. Borrowing design ideas from the native Indians and using looms brought from the Old World, Spanish weavers produced sturdy, simple blankets, serapes, and window coverings that they used to ward off the cold of mountain nights. Merchants along the trade routes learned of the woven goods and, realizing there was a potential market, soon distributed the textiles throughout the developing nation.

Although many variations emerged, the one item in greatest demand was the Rio Grande blanket, a simple striped and banded blanket longer than it was wide. Since the European looms were limited in width, two smaller blankets were sometimes sewn together to form a larger unit suitable for use as blanket or floor covering.

The Saltillo pattern, designed in Mexico for wealthy landowners, found its way to the looms of the Northern Frontier. Its diamond-shaped central motif, varying from one weaver to another, provided pleasing relief from austere furnishings. Combined with the stripes of the forerunner Rio Grande, this design became known as the Chimayo style.

As trade and communication increased, so did the weavers' designs. Eight-point stars, zigzags, pictorials, and modern motifs reflected the diversity of the weavers' talents. The woven crafts, created for utilitarian purposes but reflecting the subtle colors of the desert landscape, gained worldwide acclaim as objects of art collected by many and displayed in galleries and museums throughout the world.

WOOD CARVERS

With only the most basic woodworking tools, Spanish settlers carved the soft woods of surrounding forests into chairs, tables, benches, shelves, and sideboards for their frontier homes. The work was laborious and slow but the rough-hewn designs filled a void created by the high cost and scarcity of imported furnishings.

In comparison to their 16th Century Spanish prototypes, Colonial pieces were coarse and bulky due to the brittle nature of the soft woods from which they were made and because of the difficulty in obtaining metal, the use of decorative ironware was limited and routinely replaced by smaller, locally forged locks and hinges.

Although stocky and cumbersome, the handcrafted furniture was refined with simple carvings of botanical, native, or Moorish origin. Of particular interest were the cornstalk and step patterns used on chair posts and rails. Reminiscent of traditional Pueblo pottery and weaving symbols of rain and the heavens, these particular motifs reflected the intimate, although sometimes turbulent, relationship between settler and native.

When the railroad arrived in Santa Fe in the late 1800s, new tools and materials became available permitting an even wider range of design and technique. A bolder, more colorful style evolved. The ease of travel made possible by the railroad resulted in an influx of non-Hispanic travelers which, in turn, created new markets for the carpenters. The travelers, however, desired more innovative designs and patterns. The carvers reacted to their wishes and within a relatively short time, the chests, cabinets, and tables that served the colonists' utilitarian needs so well became eagerly sought-after commodities.

STRAW APPLIQUÉ

Sixteenth Century European wood carvers used a method known as marquetry to decorate the boxes, chests, and sconces they created. The process involved using small pieces of wood, ivory, tortoise shell, or gold either set into shallow cavities (inlay) or applied as a thin sheet to the surface (appliqué). The wood carvers of the Northern Frontier wanted their creations to be as attractive and ornamental as those of their European counterparts but, although a small amount of ivory and gold found its way into the colonies, materials to achieve the identical effect were lacking. The solution was to use readily available resources such as cornhusks and straw.

To accentuate the ornamentation, many artists painted the wood with indigo, vermilion, or lampblack. Large pieces of straw or cornhusk were split, flattened, and cut into the desirable shape. Early artists most commonly selected floral or geometric designs. The cut pieces were then glued to the painted surface and sealed with a coat of pine pitch varnish or resin. The finished product took on the appearance of gold and almost glistened in sunlight.

As the technique gained popularity, other carved objects, such as candlesticks, frames, and crosses, were added. Even so, when less complicated, more durable, means of decoration became available, the art of straw appliqué lost momentum and died out.

In the early 1930s, the Works Progress Administration (WPA) was formed to provide jobs for the able-bodied unemployed. Part of this program included grants such as the Federal Art Project (FAP) that promoted American art, painting, sculpture, handicrafts, and folk art. Several artists in New Mexico took part in Art Project and gave new life to a largely forgotten tradition. Today, straw appliqué is considered one of the finest examples of traditional Hispanic New Mexican art.

TIN SMITHS

Rumors of great wealth and cities built of gold brought Coronado and his soldiers to the Northern Frontier. They found neither, but they continued their search. In 1546, a large deposit of silver was discovered in Mexico but little, if any, ever reached the Northern Frontier. In 1598, Onate brought silversmiths into the frontier but his hunt for gold and silver was as unrewarding as previous expeditions. Aside from the few silver household items brought by settlers that arrived with Onate and de Vargas, the probability of finding silver was unlikely. Finding themselves fundamentally out of work, most silversmiths turned to blacksmithing.

When the Santa Fe Trail opened more than two hundred years later, the first annual caravan from the emergent United States arrived in New Mexico. American peddlers exchanged trade goods with the colonists. Among the goods was British tinplate, the poor man's silver. The smiths saw this as an opportunity to produce decorative furnishings at minimal cost.

Employing skills learned from their ancestors, the new artists crafted religious articles that included crosses, candlesticks, and retablos as well as chandeliers, sconces, mirrors, lanterns, and frames. Many of the ornate frames held religious prints and some of the deepest included nichos inside which the faithful inserted flowers or personal keepsakes. Almost all of the pieces were created utilizing hand stamping, punching and cutting techniques to produce unique objects of extraordinary beauty

Due to war rations and foreign imports, this art was temporarily threatened but, fortunately, is now enjoying a revival.

NATIVE POTTERY

The indigenous Indians of the Northern Frontier were an integral part of the colonists' lives. Without the Indians, the colonists might not have survived. The natives showed the newcomers how to live off the land, plant crops that would thrive in an inhospitable climate, and preserve the yield of their harvests in pottery made from the soil in which the plants grew.

The prehistoric Hohokam, Mogollon, and Anasazi Indians were producing pottery more than 2000 years ago. Crude in form and heavy in weight the cumbersome utensils served their purpose. By the time the Spaniards reached the Northern Frontier, the craft was refined and improved so that, aside from being strictly utilitarian, the pieces achieved decorative and ceremonial status.

Always formed by hand, never thrown on a wheel, local variations in clay determined the color and consistency of the pottery. Some pieces were dark red or gray, others, like those of the Picuris people, were flecked with mica. Although earlier cultures used simple geometric and curvilinear themes to decorate their pottery, the Pueblo People embellished their pieces with dots, triangles, frets, and life-form motifs.

Influenced by subsequent cultures, the pottery of the Pueblo People has seen a great amount of innovation and transformation. Today, contemporary themes are displayed alongside traditional and a wider variety of form and decoration is being utilized. However, the tradition of pottery making continues to be a heritage passed down from generation to generation. It is a tradition that echoes the beliefs of the People— to live in harmony with the earth and not exploit it.

THE PRESENT

As in past generations, the people presently living along the High Road till the soil, raise their families, and distance themselves from the outside world. Unlike nearby Santa Fe or Taos, there are no mega-malls, movie theatres, or high-rise hotels here but there are mom and pop grocery stores, produce stands, and gas stations where attendants offer to pump gas and wash windshields. Following time-honored traditions, artisans take inspiration from their ancestors and surroundings and produce amazing tinwork, carpentry, textiles, and pottery. Farmers grow crops and shepherds tend flocks. These are people who adapted to their environment and made the best of it.

Not surprisingly, religion continues to play a crucial role in the lives of the people who live here. Almost every town has a small adobe church, usually filled with Santos created by past and present Santeros. The Penitentes are present, as well, although their activities are somewhat subdued.

The history of the people along the High Road is evident in their labors. Whether they work with wood, tin, textiles, food, or animals they tell their stories and express their uniqueness; some are traditional, others contemporary.

Change is inevitable in most societies but, thankfully for the rest of us, it has been slow coming to the towns Along the High Road.

PART II

TOWNS ALONG THE HIGH ROAD

SANTA CRUZ

SANTA CRUZ DE LA CAÑADA

In 1695, Governor Diego de Vargas founded his first town, Santa Cruz de la Cañada, designed to protect the Spanish frontier north of Santa Fe. The church, which still stands, was constructed in the 1730s. In 1837, residents revolted against Mexican authorities, resulting in the death of Governor Albino Pérez.

Founded:

> Originally settled in 1598
> Abandoned in 1680
> Resettled in 1695

Original Name (1695)

> La Villa Nueva de Santa Cruz de los Espanoles Mejicanos
> del Rey Nuestro Senor Carlo Segundo - or-
> La Villa Nueva de Santa Cruz de la Canada

Location:

> 2 miles east of Espanola
> Off State Road 76

The Santa Cruz of today is a strange juxtaposition of old and new. A suburb of nearby Espanola, Santa Cruz has all the conveniences: gas stations, auto repair shops, grocers, restaurants, and a very unique taco stand. It is also at the beginning of the High Road and is, therefore, the last vestige of urbanization before heading into the frontier lands. Even so, the town retains it historic significance as the second of the three royal villas declared by the Spanish Crown and it is this history that makes the town worthy of note.

Although the settlers built a church when they and Onate arrived in the early 1600s, the church suffered extensive damage during the Pueblo Revolt of 1680 and the twelve years following. According to Governor Cervasio Cruzat y Gongora who inspected the church in 1732, it was "beyond repair and in danger of collapsing." In 1733, the settlers of La Villa Nueva de Santa Cruz obtained official permission to build a new church on land donated by a wealthy widow.

It took fifteen years to complete construction but by 1748, the colonists had a church described by Bishop Pedro Tamaron y Romeral, the Bishop of Durango, as "large and sumptuous but will little adornment." Fray Andres Garcia, assigned to Santa Cruz during the years 1765 and 1768, remedied the lack of adornment.

One of the first recognized Santeros, Garcia was a wood carver and painter noted for his tendency to paint distant objects very blue and near objects very red. He was also one of the first Santeros to paint on wood covered with yeso (gesso), a technique believed borrowed from the Pueblo Indians. Church documents indicate that, while in Santa Cruz, Garcia created a decorative altar rail, a variety of carved images, and an altar screen that is presently the focal point of the church.

The uppermost panels of the altar screen include images of the Holy Family with San Joaquin and Santa Ana (parents of the Virgin Mary) on the left; La Santa Cruz (the Holy Cross shown without the body of Christ but adorned with straw "Weapons of Christ" used in His victory against sin) in the center; and two angels on the right. The lower panel includes Santa Teresa (patron of faith) with a dove far left; Saint Joseph (adoptive father of Christ) with Santo Nino (Christ child) near left; Cristo Crucificado (Christ Crucified) in the center; San Francisco Javier (patron of missionaries) near right; and Santa Barbara (protectress against thunder and lightning) far right. At the very top of the altar screen is a dove (symbol of the Holy Spirit). The stencil work along the bottom and sides is attributed to a later Santero who renovated the altar screen.

In a commemorative publication written for the church's 300th anniversary, Father Ron Carrillo stated, "We have endured times of struggle, of religious growth and of conversion. We have endured times of war and times of peace. We have endured times of colonization and times of independence. This is precisely how our church community of 300 years was established."

On the edge of the civilized Frontier, threatened by Indian attack, and overwhelmed by isolation, the people of Santa Cruz built a church that has survived the plague of time. It is a testament to their strength and courage.

What to see:

La Iglesia Santa Cruz de la Canada (Church and Santos). While in the church, seek out the Santo Entierro (Christ in the Coffin) set into an alcove on the south side of the church. Be sure to call ahead for hours church is open. 505-753-3345.

What to look for:

Retablos and Bultos in the church

Where to eat:

El Paragua—"One of the last places you can still get authentic Mexican cuisine in a truly authentic atmosphere"
Open daily 11am to 9pm
602 Santa Cruz Road (SR76)
505-753-3211
www.elparagua.com

Some kids sell lemonade; Larry and Pete Atencio decided to sell their mother's tacos and tamales. The boys set up a table, their father supplied an umbrella to shade the boys from New Mexico's hot sun, word about the boys under the umbrella (el paraqua) got around, and a new business was born.

Everyone loved Mrs. Atencio's cooking so, in 1966, the Atencios converted the tack room of their family home into a restaurant. The following year, the family-owned plumbing shop next door was taken over to make room for a bar. The additions and expansions have continued over the years and the Atencios still devote their time to bringing Mexican dishes to old and new guests.

While dining at El Paragua, stroll outside and see the 300-year-old Alamo (cottonwood) tree. This giant of the valley boasts a 30-foot circumference. Also worth seeing is the mural of Virgen de Guadalupe, Patroness of the Americas, executed by Santa Fe artist Garduno. It is on the east outside wall by the parking lot. If you don't have time for a sit-down meal, try the El Parasol Taco Stand next to the restaurant. The food is of the same high quality and service is prompt.

Where to stay:

Inn at Santa Cruz
207 SR 76
Santa Cruz, NM
505-753-1142

Originally a stagecoach stop along Camino Real, the main route between Santa Fe and Taos, this charming adobe hacienda dates back to 1810. Set back off the road on the way to Chimayo, cross an old wooden bridge and enter a different time. Relax in the courtyard by the fountain and 300-year-old tamarisk tree. Walk the spectacular grounds with its trees, roses, goldfish pond, walking trail, and seasonal outdoor pool. Listen to the birds in the trees that surround and shelter the inn from the outside world. All seasons have something wonderful to offer.

PERSONAL NOTES:

CHIMAYO

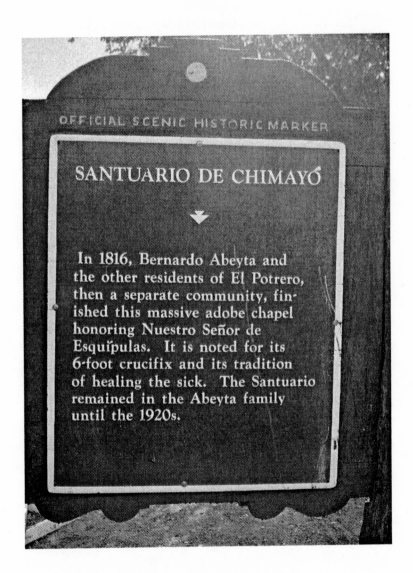

OFFICIAL SCENIC HISTORIC MARKER

SANTUARIO DE CHIMAYÓ

In 1816, Bernardo Abeyta and the other residents of El Potrero, then a separate community, finished this massive adobe chapel honoring Nuestro Señor de Esquípulas. It is noted for its 6-foot crucifix and its tradition of healing the sick. The Santuario remained in the Abeyta family until the 1920s.

Founded:

Originally settled around 1598
Abandoned in 1680
Resettled after 1692

Original Name:

Tzimayo (Pueblo name meaning "good flaking stone")
San Buenaventura de Chimayo

Location:

11 miles east of Espanola
On State Road 76

One day may not be enough time to take in all that Chimayo offers. Even though this village is world famous for its chiles, weaving, and the sacred earth of the Santuario de Chimayo, its secrets and legends are hidden as only the most observant traveler will discover.

The first people to occupy the area were Tewa Indians. One of their ancient legends recounts a battle between twin war gods and an evil monster that devoured children. The battle lasted several days, but the war gods finally won out. As the fiendish creature died, the earth began to smoke, and flames rose from deep within a pond the Indians called Tsimayo-pokwi. Because good had overcome evil in this place, the Indians considered it a source of great healing and used its waters both to cure and ward off various illnesses. Eventually the water evaporated and turned to mud, but the healing practices continued. Even when the mud finally turned to dust, the Indians traveled great distances just to rub some of the health-giving soil on their ailing bodies.

Hundreds of years later, Spanish colonists moved into the area. Located on the eastern boundary of the Northern Frontier, the new settlement was regarded as the outermost edge of civilization. Its mountains and hills were treacherous and isolated, the weather was characterized by heavy rains and cold winds, and the Indians whispered about formidable giants living in the numerous caves that dotted the landscape. What better place to confine vagabonds, gypsies, antisocials, and degenerates? Although no official record of an incarceration location exists, historians believe these reprobates, often forced into servitude and military conscription, occupied the Tzimayo Valley until the Pueblo Revolt of 1680.

Sometime after the Revolt, settlers moved back into the area. Threatened by continued hostile Indian attack and fearing for their lives, the colonists built their homes around a defensible central plaza, the Plaza de San Buenaventura, now known as Plaza del Cerro. With only three entranceways into the compound, the homes faced inward toward the main square. Families and animals were sheltered within the compound's walls and a life-giving acequia (ditch) ran through the center of the plaza. In recent years, the Chimayo Cultural Preservation Association has restored the Plaza del Cerro and inaugurated the Chimayo Museum to sustain and promote the culture and traditions of this historic northern New Mexico community.

In an area probably used as pastureland, another settlement developed. Known as Potrero, this settlement was the home of Don Bernardo Abeyta, an honored member of the Penitentes who, as legend records, discovered a mysterious crucifix near his home.

On a Good Friday in the early 1800s, Don Bernardo left his home in Potrero to perform the society's traditional penances near the ancient Indian pond. On the way, he was startled by a sudden burst of light. Though frightened at first, Don Bernardo realized that the light was coming from the ground just a few feet ahead. Thinking it might be lost gold from the fabled Seven Cities of Cibola, he fell to his knees and started digging with his bare hands. What he found was a six-foot-tall, dusky-green crucifix bearing a dark-skinned corpus. Abeyta immediately recognized the crucifix as that of the Black Christ, Our Lord of Esquipulas, which had first been brought to the area by a Guatemalan priest more than a century earlier. During the Pueblo Revolt, the priest had been killed and his body buried along with the cross.

Overwhelmed by the discovery, Don Bernardo rubbed his dirt-stained hands across his face and body. Later he would tell neighbors that the soil in which the crucifix had been buried cured him of an ongoing illness; but for the time being, his only concern was to notify the local priest, Father Sebastian Alvarez.

Father Alvarez took the crucifix back to his church in Santa Cruz and installed it in a place of honor on the main altar. The next morning when he went into the church to say Mass, the crucifix was gone. Fearing the worst, he set out to tell Don Bernardo that the crucifix had been stolen. But before reaching Abeyta's hacienda, he noticed a group of people gathered around the place where the crucifix had been found.

"What is going on?" he asked. The people stood back and pointed to the ground. The crucifix had returned.

Once again, Father Alvarez transported the crucifix to the church in Santa Cruz, and once again, it reappeared where it had been found. After yet a third futile attempt, it was agreed that the crucifix belonged in Potrero.

Abeyta built a hermita (small shelter) over the holy ground, leaving a pozito (hole) in the floor so that others could touch the tierra bendita (holy earth) and perhaps be healed as he had been. With permission from the church in Santa Cruz, he began construction of a chapel to house the crucifix.

Two rooms, one to the left and one to the right, formed the narthex (vestibule) of the chapel. Within the nave or main body of the church, were bultos (carvings) and retablos (paintings) depicting saints, liturgical feasts, and members of the Holy

Family. Behind the main altar, the treasured crucifix was surrounded by a large reredos (altar screen) variously depicting the Jerusalem Cross, the Franciscan emblem, and a cross with a lance, rod, heart, and the four wounds of Christ. To the left of the altar was the original hermita with the pozito for the tierra bendita, and a prayer room. It took several years to complete construction, but by 1816, El Santuario de Nuestro Senor de Esquipulas was finished.

El Santuario remained a privately owned chapel until 1929 when, after much neglect and financial difficulties, title to the property was transferred to the Archdiocese of Santa Fe. Under the careful direction of the priests of the Congregation of Sons of the Holy Family, El Santuario was restored. As more and more people came to worship in front of the large crucifix

and to seek the healing power of the earth, more and more accounts of miraculous cures were added to that of Abeyta's. Since that time, El Santuario has been designated a National Historic Landmark and is frequently referred to as the "Lourdes of America" because of its similarity to the famous shrine in France.

It has been said that the discarded canes, braces, wheelchairs, and messages of thanksgiving that hang from the adobe walls in the prayer room are proof of the miracles of Chimayo. Still, while many people have left their crutches and walked away cured, the Catholic Church has never sought to officially confirm or deny any of the miracles. It has also been said that the dirt in the pozito replenishes itself. Yet, it is common knowledge that the dirt is brought in from surrounding hillsides and, though blessed by a priest, has no special power in and of itself.

Regardless of the controversy, El Santuario remains a place of tranquility and spiritual renewal to which thousands of people travel during Holy Week, on Mother's Day or on other significant occasions throughout the year.

Leaving the Santuario, pilgrims can take a short walk to visit a smaller, lesser known, chapel, that of El Santo Nino de Atocha (the Holy Child of Atocha). There are conflicting legends and opinions as to the origin of the statue that graces this chapel. Some people say it was found in the ground, like the crucifix in the Santuario, while others believe it was given in response to a parishioner's request. Either way, it is said the statue of Santo Nino de Atocha, had a life of its own and often disappeared from its shrine only to return with its feet wet and its shoes worn out. These sojourns usually occurred at night and involved the saint walking around the countryside to help people, especially children, who were sick or troubled. As a form of propitiation, baby shoes were placed before the statue in order that the Santo might continue its good work.

In her book *Chimayo Valley Traditions*, Elizabeth Kay states: "The Santo Nino de Atocha became the patron saint of prisoners and travelers in New Mexico. Settlers in northern New Mexico were frequently threatened by roving bands of Indians, much as the Christian Spanish had been by the Moors in the Middle Ages. The frequent kidnapping of Spanish children and adults by Indian raiders increased the settler's devotion to the Holy Child and stories about His rescuing people from captivity were common in New Mexico in the nineteenth and even the twentieth centuries."

Severiano Medina built the chapel that houses El Santo Nino de Atocha in 1857. His wife, Saranita, provided baby shoes, free of charge, to those wishing to make a pilgrimage to the Holy Child's shrine. Upon their deaths in 1985, only months apart, both Severiano and Saranita were buried, side-by-side, in the chapel's courtyard. However, to this day, in the true Hispanic tradition, the placing of baby shoes around the statue continues.

In the trees around the chapels, a large black and white bird makes its presence known. Flitting from tree to tree or hopping around on the ground, the Black-billed Magpie emits a distinctive, almost ear piercing, "yak-yak-yak." An aggressive thief of the countryside, this bird steals its food from birdfeeders, other birds' nests, nearby orchards, even Cujo's dog dish. Even so, it is a sight not to be missed. With a tail as long as its body, luminous black head and breast, and stark white belly and shoulders, it adds charm and allure to an already enchanting landscape.

After their journey through the sanctuaries of El Potrero, many travelers choose to visit the shops of numerous artists where they can view, and purchase, religious items, paintings, wood carvings, and the renowned Chimayo-style woven rugs.

Three families are credited with the establishment of an industry that brought industry and fame to the Chimayo Valley. The Ortega, Cordova, and Trujillo families produced blankets, serapes, and rugs from wool sheared from locally raised sheep. Originally created for utilitarian use, the high quality of the textiles and the reputation of their weavers caught the attention of Santa Fe curio dealers. The rugs and blankets were unique and affordable—two attributes the dealers found desirable. The opening of the Santa Fe Trail and the arrival of the railroad made widespread distribution possible.

Over the years the demand grew, the weavers increased the variety of their production to include wall hangings, table runners, pillow tops, and clothing, and the industry thrived.

The countryside around the Chimayo Valley is rich and fertile and provides the perfect growing medium for chiles, a trademark of northern New Mexico. Roadside stands, grocery stores, restaurants, even adobe homes, all sing the praises of the chile. For most New Mexicans, the Chile is a noble being and a day with chile is like a day without sunshine. And whether the choice is green or red, it can be found in Chimayo. So, before leaving, try a plateful of enchiladas or tacos topped with the fiery condiment. Or better yet, order some Green Chile Stew. What better way to round out a trip to the Chimayo Valley!

What to see:
El Santuario de Nuestro Senor de Esquipulas—Open daily
El Capilla del Santo Nino de Atocha—Open daily
The Chimayo Museum and the Plaza del Cerro—Located at the Plaza del Cerro near Ortega's Weaving Shop—Call for hours—505-351-0945

The weavers' and artists' workshops—Hours vary by establishment
Chimayo Festival of Arts Studio Tour—(2nd weekend in October) Contact Maria L. Vigil, Studio Tour Director for more information, 505-351-0945

What to look for:

Santos, weavers, tinwork, chiles, and miracles.

Where to eat:

Leona's Restaurante and Gift shop
Open daily 9am to 5pm—Closed Tuesdays
On the plaza surrounding the Santuario
505-351-4569
www.leonasrestaurante.com

For more than thirty-seven years, Leona Medina-Tiede
worked night and day to perfect recipes to provide visitors
with homemade tamales, tortillas, burritos, posole and

pinto beans. She started with a small roadside stand but soon discovered that more room was needed to prepare the food for Chimayo's countless pilgrims. Her diligence and dedication paid off. Today—aside from offering visitors a hot (in more ways than one) meal—a wide variety of New Mexican chiles, tortillas, and sauces are available for sale or shipment from either the restaurant or website.

Rancho de Chimayo Restaurant and Galleries
Open daily 11:30am to 9pm (Closed Mondays November thru May)
County Road 98
505-351-4444
www.ranchochimayo.com

Down the road from the Santuario—The whole world walks through the doorway of Rancho de Chimayo. Unique New Mexican cuisine, prepared with locally grown products from recipes that have been in the family for generations. In October of 1965, grandson Arturo Jaramillo and his wife Florence transformed the ancestral home of Hermenegildo and Trinidad Jaramillo into the Restaurante Rancho de Chimayo. Today, the Rancho de Chimayo Restaurant is one of the most visited dining establishments in the world and is continually listed as one of the Top 100 Restaurant establishments in the United States.

Where to Stay

Casa Escondida Bed and Breakfast
Route 0100
505-351-4805
www.casaescondida.com

"The Hidden House," nestled on six acres of secluded land is an intimate and serene inn built in the Spanish Colonial adobe style typical of northern New Mexico. A comfortable oasis decorated in the American Arts & Crafts style. Eight exquisite rooms with private bathrooms, full breakfast, and hot tub.

El Meson de la Centinela
County Road 64
505-351-2280 (Ask for Pat)
www.centinelaranch.com

This charming adobe inn, nestled inside a working ranch with donkeys, horses, sheep, and apple orchard is situated in the heart of the Chimayo Valley Mexico and features the rich and beautiful architecture of northern New Mexico. There are three spacious casita-style suites, all with kiva fireplaces, kitchens and full baths. Across from master weavers and wood carvers, it is the perfect base for travels along the High Road.

Hacienda de Chimayo
County Road 98 (Across from Rancho de Chimayo Restaurante)
505-351-2222.
www.ranchochimayo.com

In August of 1984, the Jaramillo family completed restoration of Hacienda de Chimayo, the family home of Epifanio and Adelaida Jaramillo. Built in the adobe tradition, the home has been renovated into seven lovely guest rooms. Each guest room opens into an enclosed courtyard and within each room, one can find turn of the century antiques, a private bath, a quiet sitting area, and a fireplace. In the old world tradition, a continental breakfast awaits each guest in the morning.

La Posada de Chimayo
County Road 0101
505-351-4605
www.laposaddadechimayo.com

The first in New Mexico, this bed and breakfast is a small adobe guesthouse just off the High Road. Get a glimpse into the life of the real Northern New Mexico - Not too far removed from the past, nor too close to the future. Full breakfast, fireplaces in all rooms, guest may help themselves to wine.

Rancho Manzana
#26 Camino de Mission (County Road 94E)
505-351-2227
www.ranchomanzana.com

Located on the historic Plaza del Cerro, this was the original family residence and mercantile store for the Ortega family and dates from the mid 1700s when New Mexico was still largely unsettled. Each room has been carefully appointed. Luxurious robes, oversized towels, and down comforters are standard. The hot tub is always available for a relaxing soak. A full breakfast is served either in the kitchen, on the deck, or overlooking the gardens and orchard. Cooking classes are taught by a variety of local and nationally known chefs and feature Rancho Manzana produce.

CORDOVA

Founded:
    1749

Original Name:
    Llano (or Pueblo) Quemado (Burned Village)

Location:
    14 miles east of Espanola
    1 mile south of State Road 76

Driving down the hill from State Road 76, Cordova appears to be a town that time has forgotten. Almost hidden in the Rio Quemado Valley, its houses are old but in good repair; trucks seem to outnumber automobiles; the few people out and about are dressed in work clothes; dogs are everywhere. There is a feel about this place, almost like stepping back into time. If you listen closely, you can almost hear one of the old ones.

My name is Diego and this is my orchard. It is doing well. Soon the delicate flowers will turn to apples and then, if God blesses the trees with enough rain, the apples will grow. I remember when we first came here. That was what...forty years ago?

It was in 1838, a year after the people in Santa Cruz and Chimayo got together to fight the governor's new taxation plan. We didn't think honest, hard-working people should have to go to jail just because they couldn't afford to pay the new taxes. Didn't the governor already have enough money? And that church in Santa Cruz. It is so big! Why do God-fearing people need a church that big? Do they think God doesn't hear prayers from the small churches and family altars? But it was terrible what happened to the Governor. The Indians shouldn't have cut his head off like that. He was only following the orders of his superiors. It seemed like the world was going crazy and that was the reason I moved to Llano Quemado where my family could live peacefully.

True, the first years were difficult. There was no money and we had to grow, make, or barter for everything we owned. But that was all right because no one else in the valley had money either. We did the best we could.

Don Bernardo Abeyta from Potrero built our chapel in 1832. Dedicated to San Antonio de Padua, the finder of lost articles and patron of animals, the church was small but so was the village. Jose Rafael Aragon, an artist originally from Santa Fe but now living in the Llano, painted the altar screens. They are wonderful to look at. Every year on June 13th, the padre comes from Santa Cruz and rings the bell in the tower so that everyone knows to come in from the fields to celebrate San Antonio's Feast day. Aside from Sundays and Holy days it is the only time everyone gets together. They crowd into the church, sometimes filling the choir loft, and those who come late stand outside with the animals. There is a Mass, a procession, music, and lots of good food. It lasts all day, well into the dark. Sometimes the men drink too much and get rowdy but they go to confession the following Saturday and God forgives them their sins.

Many of the men in the village belong to the brotherhood, the Penitentes as they are called. On Good Friday, one of them carries a cross to the top of the hill to remember Christ's suffering and death. When the new Bishop arrived in Santa Fe, he said the Penitentes were bad and that our statues were sacrilegious. Now we hide the statues and the Penitentes only go out when they know no one is around. The Hermano Mayor asked if I wished to become a Penitente. I even went to one of the meetings at the morada. But it is a difficult life that demands a lot of sacrifice and I worry about my family. So, I said "no thank you."

My neighbor, Francisco, is a carpintero. He made some of the Santos for our little chapel. It was Francisco that convinced me that I, too, could be a wood carver. Francisco showed me how to use the adze and other tools used to craft the Santos. I made a couple of small Santos for our family altar. My wife, Teresa, liked them but they weren't good enough for the church. That's when I started making furniture.

First, I made a table. I carved some flowers on the legs and smoothed the top until it shined. Then I had to make the chairs to go with the table. One of our neighbors saw the table and chairs and asked if I could make a set for his wife. He said he would give me four sheep if I finished the work before Christmas. It was slow work but, eventually, I finished. After that, another neighbor asked about a trastero. I wasn't sure about making it but Francisco helped out and, soon, that was finished, also. People came from other villages and asked about my furniture. Now I have more work than I can handle. But I also have a lot of sheep, so that is a good thing.

My wife Teresa is a good woman even though she believes brujas live in the trees and evil spirits ride on the wind. But those things don't matter to me because she makes the best tortillas in the valley, sews my pants when I wear holes in them, and raises our children to respect their family, the earth, and all of God's creatures. She also helps during lambing season and when we shear the sheep. Right now, she is pregnant with our fifth child. Two children, both girls, have already been taken to heaven - they are the angels that watch over the rest of the family. The two boys that remain are strong and healthy. I don't know if they will want to be wood carvers or if they will even stay on the land. No matter what else, they have to be themselves. Maybe our next child will just work with the sheep or in the orchard. It is hard to tell. But I will teach my children whatever they wish to learn when they are ready—they are the future of this valley. Maybe times will be better for them.

And so, it was, and still is, in this tiny village. To this day, fathers pass down centuries-old traditions to sons and daughters, mothers continue to cook, sew, and raise families, and the old church still stands, almost hidden by the old adobe houses that surround it.

Except for a long-ago forest fire that gave this village its original name, nothing of great importance happened here—no battles won or lost, no discovery of gold, no recorded miracles. A few artists sell exquisite wood carvings here but there are no bed and breakfasts or restaurants to be found. This is a town of

down-to-earth, hard-working people whose traditions, hearts, and spirits have helped them make sense of a complicated world.

Has time forgotten this village or merely been gentle to it?

What to see:

San Antonio de Padua Church—Closed except for services
Rural countryside.

What to look for:

Woodcarvings—furniture, Santos, small animals.

Where to eat:

The closest restaurants are in Chimayo.

Where to stay:

The closet accommodations are in Chimayo.

PERSONAL NOTES:

TRUCHAS

Founded:

Around 1752

Officially granted Royal possession on April 24, 1754

Original Name:

Nuestra Senora del Rosario, San Fernando y Santiago del Rio de las Truchas (Our Lady of the rosary, Saints Ferndinad of Spain and James the Greater, of the River of the Trout)

Location:

20 miles east of Espanola

On State Road 76

By the mid 1700s, hostile Indian attacks became a serious problem for the small villages scattered along the High Road. In an effort to create a defensive outpost, the Royal government offered free land to settlers that agreed to move to a high mesa north of Cordova. The new settlement would act as a defensive outpost that would improve security in the valley villages. However, in order to secure title to the property, settlers had to occupy and work the land for a period of two years. It was a daunting proposition, but twelve families accepted the challenge. They went to work, built homes, raised farm animals, dug acequias, and planted crops.

The Royalty's plan worked like fuel to a fire. Instead of dwindling, the Indian attacks intensified. The village was easy prey for the Indians who hid in the mountain passes. Often sneaking down in the dark of night, they raided the fields, stole livestock, and terrorized the colonists. When the settlers asked for guns and military aid, their requests were denied because officials in Santa Fe didn't have the troops or equipment to provide them the protection they needed. As in the past, the colonists were on their own.

Successfully transforming disaster into success, at the end of the requisite two years the settlers petitioned Governor Tomas Velez Cachupin and, as part of the 1754 Rosario Land Grant, achieved official status as the new 15,000-acre settlement of Nuestra Senora del Rosario, San Fernando y Santiago del Rio de las Truchas.

According to archived documents, of the twelve families that petitioned for the land grant, six were named Romero and four were named Espinosa. A coincidence? Hardly. It was common for extended families to relocate as a group. In their new location, grandparents, aunts, uncles, parents, and children worked long hours planting and harvesting crops, putting up fences, caring for livestock, and defending their homes. Maybe, more than anything else, the one factor that assured their success was the settlers' sense of family unity.

Family was more than just a word to the Northern Frontier colonists - it was a way of life. Several generations of a family lived together, worked together, prayed together, and survived or perished together. Siblings obeyed their parents, and the parents respected and gained wisdom from their elders. As a cultural entity, the family preserved its language, religion, customs, and traditions. The importance of being connected to family was the basis of their identity.

Although the elders functioned as hierarchal leaders, aunts and uncles might be padrinos (godparents), while cousins and other extended family members might be compadres (friends or co-parents) that provided mutual aid whenever necessary. Everything revolved around the family and every member of the family served a purpose. Without the family, or religion, there was nothing.

It wasn't until the early 1800s, however, that the people of Truchas were able to build a church of their own. Appropriately named Nuestra Senora del Rosario, the church, situated in the center of the village and enclosed in a walled yard, contains magnificent examples of early Santero work. As was the tradition, most of the pieces are unsigned although two altar screens reveal the date and identity of their creator, Pedro Antonio Fresquis. When the roof and bell tower collapsed in the late 1800s, the residents of Truchas feared for the survival of the artwork. They re-roofed the church in 1878 then added a metal corrugated roof in 1900.

In the 1970s, a new church was built a couple of miles away on the road leading out of the village but Holy Week services are still held at the old church. Today, the church of Nuestra Senora del Rosario stands as a testament of the love and devotion of the people who put their faith in God and endured the ordeal and isolation of New Mexico's Northern Frontier.

John Nichols' book, The Milagro Beanfield War, characterized the family values, religious beliefs, and unity of the people in a New Mexico town he called Milagro (Miracle); Robert Redford gave them life in his movie version filmed in Truchas. Sometimes humorous, sometimes heartbreaking, the book and movie both give insight into life, past and present, along the High Road. An old man talks to saints; Death, "decked out in a sombrero, a serape, and shiny silver spurs" hangs around the village; a young man rebels against the "dominant" society; a Vista volunteer is bowled over by all he sees or thinks he sees. Yet, in the end, everyone comes together and life continues, as in the past.

In 1996, Max Cordova, a long time resident of Truchas, took up where his fictional predecessor left off. When environmentalists won a lawsuit again the Forest Service, strict wood-gathering restrictions were put into effect radically limiting the amount of wood residents could take from the forest. The environmentalists' argument was that tall trees, the preferred habitat of the Mexican spotted owl (an endangered species), were being cut and that the future of the spotted owl was in jeopardy. According to the original land grant, the land and the trees on it belonged to the residents of the village. Cordova believed the new restrictions favored the owl.

Although numerous recommendations were made for the creation of a sustainable fuel wood management plan, none were ever implemented. Push came to shove and the environmentalists were the ones doing the pushing. As wood was the only energy source available for winter heating and cooking, Cordova led Truchas villagers in a protest that quickly developed into a quagmire. The villagers shoved back.

For a while, things were tense in the small village. Angry residents hung two of the environmentalists in effigy and made threats on the lives of others. A compromise was reached that allowed residents to cut small green trees in overgrown areas thereby preserving the spotted owls' habitat, reducing fire danger, and giving villagers enough wood fuel to meet their needs. Only time will tell whether the plan works or not.

As entertaining or compelling as they might be, books, movies, and civil suits are not Truchas' only claims to fame. There are other, more vigorous things that draw visitors to this area—like the mountains.

Although not the highest mountains in the state, Wheeler Peak is higher at 13,160 feet, the Truchas Peaks dominate the landscape and lure hikers and climbers to their summits. Somewhat difficult to locate, Middle Truchas Peak (13,070 feet) and South Truchas Peak, (13,102 feet) can be accessed via an 8.5 mile-long gravel road that leads out from the village. The trails to North Truchas Peak (13,024 feet) and West Truchas (13,066 feet) are more elusive and require the use of a good topographical map. A word of caution about hiking in New Mexico: Know what you're doing, make sure someone knows where you are going, never hike alone, get an early start, take plenty of water, leave no trace, and be prepared for the unexpected. Enough said.

The less adventurous folk will enjoy the many galleries in Truchas. During an annual event held on the last two weekends in September, the Fiesta de Cultura y Cosecha features the work of artists from Truchas as well as Chimayo, Ojo Sarco, Chamisal, and Penasco. Artists open their studios, music and the aroma of good food fills the air, and traditions are made and preserved. It is a rare glimpse into the lives of these hardy people—one not to be missed.

What to see:

Nuestra Senora del Rosario Church—Village Center

Penitente Morada—on the left as you enter town—closed to the public

The Fiesta de Cultura y Cosecha (Last 2 weekends in September) Contact the
High Road Marketplace in Chimayo at 866-804-5702

Truchas artist workshops—Hours vary by establishment

Truchas Peaks—Trailhead at east end of town. Contact the Santa Fe National Forest at 505-438-7840

What to look for:

Old farms, Mexican spotted owls, things other people don't see. There's also a gas station and general store in case you need provisions.

Where to eat:

The closest restaurants are in Chimayo and Picuris.

Where to stay:

Rancho Arriba Bed & Breakfast
Off of State Road 76
505-689-2374
www.ranchoarriba.com

Lying at the edge of the Carson National Forest at an elevation of 8400 feet, this working farm/bed & breakfast offers rural tranquility and informal charm to those seeking a unique retreat. Four rooms in the adobe hacienda and guest wing provide guests the opportunity to live a true frontiersman life—if only for one night. A full, family-style breakfast, cooked on a woodstove completes the experience.

Rancho del Llano
371 County Road 0078
505-689-2347

Queen size beds, microwaves, TVs, and private baths are only a few of the amenities this bed & breakfast offers. There are hiking trails and cookout areas on the property as well as clean, comfortable stalls for travelers' horses. As if that weren't enough, there are also magnificent views, spectacular sunsets, a library of Southwestern books, and a complete northern New Mexico-style breakfast. This is a gem hidden in the mountains.

Truchas Farmhouse Inn
Off State Road 76
505-689-2245

Sit by the pond and look for trout. Imagine what life was like in the late 1700s. Gaze at the Truchas Peaks and visualize yourself climbing them. Then spend the evening in front of a warm fire and fall asleep to the sound of complete silence. This is what you will find at this small inn. It's not fancy but it is definitely charming.

PERSONAL NOTES:

OJO SARCO

Founded:
>   Late 1800s-exact date unknown

Original Name:
>   Diamante
>   Ojo Zarco (1912)

Location:
>   22 miles east of Espanola
>   West of State Road 76

Very little is known about this small village 6 miles north of Truchas and 2 miles west of State Road 76. Its original name was Diamante (diamond), possibly after a founding family or because it is a jewel in the rough, but the name was changed to Ojo Zarco (possible misspelling) in 1912, and current residents refer to it as Ojo Sarco (clear or visible stream).

The village itself is a relic of the past with small farms strung along two side roads that meet at the highway. Many of the old adobe homes date back to the late 1800s when villagers from nearby Las Trampas moved here in the hope of finding more land and room to move around. Some of the houses are more recent, however, built by artists and writers that now call this village home.

In 1886, the villagers of Diamante built a church in honor of their patron saint, Santo Tomas Apostol (the Doubting Thomas) who was martyred in India while working to convert the nonbelievers, a fate many padres suffered during the early days of New Mexico's Northern Frontier. The church is a morada-like adobe structure, with few windows, a corrugated metal roof, and a single bell tower. Inside are vigas (log roof beams), wood floors, and a latticed-wood altar rail. On July 3, parishioners celebrate Santo Tomas's feast day with a procession through the dusty roads of the village, possibly asking that the saint bring faith and trust to those in need.

As the population grew, the need for a school became evident. Sometime in the 1940s, an elementary school was built. Two teachers who used books donated by the Michigan public school system taught all eight grades. The only problem was that most of the students were Hispanic and spoke little or no English.

Even if the children could have read the books, the subject matter held no relevancy to students born and raised in the mountains of New Mexico. The teachers solved the dilemma by teaching the ABC's, grammar, and penmanship on that old standby, the blackboard.

When Kathy Riggs visited Santa Fe in 1973, she took a pottery workshop and soon realized she had the talent, dedication, and patience necessary to create clay works. After a lengthy apprenticeship, she set up a studio, did some experimenting, and began selling her work. Following a stint in the Peace Corps Jake Willson completed a degree in economics and public administration, and then decided he needed a change of pace. He moved to Ojo Sarco, met Kathy, married her, and helped build the business they call Ojo Sarco Pottery.

The pottery Kathy and Jake produce is unlike any other in New Mexico. Its lines are clean and abstract and its glazes replicate the colors of the landscape—vibrant and ever changing. No two pieces are alike as each piece is individually crafted and fired. The work is arduous but the results are amazing, reflecting the diversity and multicultural heritage of this unique region.

One writer mistakenly called Ojo Sarco a ghost town. If he had taken more time, he would have discovered that the people of Ojo Sarco are alive and well, living peacefully Along the High Road.

What to see:
> Santo Tomas Apostol Church
> Artists' workshops—Hours vary
> Ojo Sarco Pottery—Open 10am to 5pm daily
> Call 505-689-2354
> www.ojosarco.com

The High Road Art Tour—Last 2 weekends in September—Featuring sculpture, jewelry, pottery and more—Call 505-351-1078 for more information. www.highroadnewmexico.com

What to look for:
See if you can find the old schoolhouse

Where to eat:
The closest restaurants are in Penasco and Picuris

Where to stay:
The closest accommodations are in Vadito

PERSONAL NOTES:

LAS TRAMPAS

Founded:

1751

Original Name:

Santo Tomas Apostol del Rio de las Trampas (Saint Thomas the Apostle of the River of Traps)

Location:

24 miles east of Espanola
On State Road 76

The life-blood of the Spanish Northern Frontier was economic growth and, toward that end, the Spanish government established a land grant system as a means of encouraging colonization. Grantees were required to step on the land, run their fingers through the soil, and make a public commitment (usually shouting four times into the wind) to live on, cultivate, and when necessary, defend the land with their lives. Seventy-four-year-old Juan de Arguello, once attached to the Presidio in Santa Fe, and the twelve families that accompanied him, did just that. In 1751, as reward for previous government service, Tomas Velez Cachupin, the forty-fifth governor of New Mexico, awarded them land that became known as Santo Tomas Apostle del Rio de las Trampas.

The grant included three types of property: private parcels for individual family use; public parcels for a church and plaza; and common lands (ejidos) composed of woodlands and meadows on which villagers hunted, gathered wood, and pastured livestock. The colonists named their village Santo Tomas Apostol del Rio de las Trampas in honor of their patron saint, Saint Thomas the Apostle, and also after a nearby river, Rio de las Trampas, the

River of Traps, so named because of the many fur traders that took beaver from its waters.

Knowing that the location of their village put them in a precarious position open to attack by marauding Indians, the colonists built thick-walled adobe homes around a central plaza. As in other villages, there were only one or two entrances to the plaza. In case of attack, livestock was hustled into the plaza center and guards, usually armed with farm tools, took defensive positions on the surrounding walls.

From the beginning, the villagers wanted a church of their own but at an altitude of 8000 feet, the growing season was short and there was little money to spare. In order to finance construction of a church they collected one-sixth of each family's annual crop earnings. In the meantime, the villagers traveled nine miles to attend Mass at the church located in Picuris Pueblo. It was a long and dangerous trip through a mountain pass filled with snow in the winter months and the threat of hostile attack in the summer. However, by 1760, they raised enough money to begin construction of their church.

The villagers did all of the construction work themselves. Women mixed adobe for bricks and plastered the outside walls; men placed the adobes, laid the wooden floor, and raised the enormous vigas into place. They built an exterior balcony for outside services and a choir loft for inside. Local Santeros created eight altar screens and numerous bultos and retablos to decorate the interior.

Originally named Santo Tomas del Rio de las Trampas but later changed to San Jose de Garcia, the church was built in the traditional cruciform style with two bell towers. The original bells were made from a combination of gold, silver, and other metals, most of which were household items brought from the Old World. The villagers loved their bells and named them. "Maria del Refugio" was rung for the death of an adult and "Maria de la

Gracia" was rung for the death of an infant. By 1776, construction of the church was complete. But something was missing—a priest.

Although a Catholic Mission was established at the Picuris Pueblo in the early 1620s, the inhabitants of Picuris were not particularly receptive to newcomers. In 1680, they murdered their resident priest, burned the existing church to the ground, and abandoned the pueblo. Somewhat subdued after the reconquest in 1696, the Picuris people returned to their pueblo and built a new church. However, knowing that the Picuris were long-time friends of the troublesome Apaches, priests feared for their lives and seldom visited either the church in Picuris or the one in nearby Las Trampas.

Like many others in their situation, the men of Las Trampas took matters into their own hands and built a morada on the back of their new church where they carried out Penitente practices. There were two divisions to the Penitente Brotherhood: the Brothers of Light and the Brothers of Blood. In the church, the Brothers of Light performed baptisms, weddings, and funerals. In the morada, the Brothers of Blood conducted rituals of penance. By the mid-1800s, a life-style of hard work, reparation, and self-determination prevailed in the village of Las Trampas. But things were about to change.

At the beginning of the Mexican American War of 1846–1848, General Stephen Watts Kearney marched 1700 troops into Santa Fe and proclaimed that the area known as New Mexico was officially a territory of the United States. Article VIII of the 1848 Treaty of Guadalupe-Hidalgo, which ended the war, stated "property of every kind...shall be inviolably respected. The present owners, the heirs of these, and all...who may hereafter acquire said property by contract, shall enjoy with respect to it, all guarantees, equally amble, as if the same belonged to citizens of the United States." Article IX further avowed "free exercise of ... religion, without restriction." Neither happened.

In 1851 when Bishop Lamy arrived in Santa Fe, he began a series of condemnations that sent Penitentes into hiding for almost 100 years. And, in 1870, a group of lawyers, businessmen, judges, and politicians joined together in a profit-making scheme to gain possession of crudely documented land parcels. In what became known as the "Santa Fe Ring," these scandalous land-grabbers ignited feuds that ended in bloodshed, hangings, even murder. Landowners were pitted against squatters. In Las Trampas, and all the other towns along the High Road, those who could not prove clear title to their land found themselves dispossessed. When the Santa Fe Ring went into bankruptcy, the U.S. Forest Service assumed responsibility for the seized land. However, to this day, ownership based on the Spanish Land Grant system is a hotly contested issue.

What to see:

San Jose de Garcia de Las Trampas Church—A National Historic Landmark Often locked except for services and feast day (March 19.) Ask local residents about gaining entry.

La Tiendita—Local and regional crafts

El Milagro—Woodcarvings and crafts

What to look for:

Santos dating back to 1776 in the church
The old morada at the rear of the church
Cattle drives in Spring and Fall
Old log flume that brings irrigation water from acequia to orchards

Where to eat:

The closest restaurants are in Picuris and Penasco

Where to stay:

The closest accommodations are in Vadito

PERSONAL NOTES:

PUEBLO of PICURIS

Founded:
    Originally settled by Anasazi around AD 750
    Occupied by Pot Creek emigrants around AD 1300

Original Name:
> Piwetha (Pass in the Mountains)
> Pikuria (Keres-Those who paint)
> San Lorenzo de Picuris (Spanish-St Lawrence of Picuris)

Location:
> 31 miles northeast of Espanola
> Off State Road 75, on Indian Road 120

Just beyond the small farming community of Chamisal, State Road 76 dead-ends at State Road 75. The village of Penasco is to the south; the Pueblo of Picuris is to the north. Although not actually on the High Road, the history, location, and pottery of Picuris makes it well worth a short detour.

The first people to live at what is now known as the Pueblo of Picuris were the Anasazi (ancestral Puebloan term probably meaning "The Old Ones".) Living in shallow caves and pithouses and subsisting on hunting and gathering, they developed a distinctive black on white pottery form used for utilitarian and trade purposes. Sometime in the late 1100s, a shift in population took place and the Anasazi relocated further south.

In an area further north, now known as the Pot Creek Pueblo, other indigenous people were planting crops and building multi-storied dwellings. As their population grew and resources diminished, they sought new land and found it in the deserted Anasazi mountain pass ruins. Calling themselves the Piwetha People, the Pot Creek emigrants continued their tradition of building apartment-like residences, some reaching five or six levels. Their numbers increased and by the time the Spanish "discovered" them, the population of the Piwetha People exceeded 3000.

Because of the village's remote mountain setting, several Spanish explorers missed locating it when they surveyed the region on earlier expeditions but in January of 1591, Castano de Sosa braved the deep snow in the treacherous mountain pass and came upon the Piwetha People. His reception was less than friendly. For more than two hundred years, the Piwetha People lived productive, independent lives, devoid of interference. They had no tolerance for strange, bearded men who rode on the backs of animals and didn't speak or understand their language. They shunned the explorer and his assemblage. Sosa reported his findings but it wasn't until 1598 that another expedition made its way into the hidden valley.

On a sunny day in July of 1598, Juan de Onate, the newly appointed governor of New Mexico, and his men entered Piwetha. Some historians speculate Onate chose Piwetha in an effort to win allies in his fight against hostile tribes; others believe he intended to carry out a Royal directive to pacify and christianize the Indians. Regardless of motive, Onate's expedition to Piwetha was a dismal failure. The Piwetha People traded with the Apaches and the religion of Onate and his men was alien to their own beliefs. Why should they, the people of the mountain pass, pray to one man-like God somewhere off in a place called Heaven when their Gods were present in everything around them? Onate saw no benefit in attempting to colonize the Piwetha People. Besides, due to their affiliation with the Apache, war was a possibility and that was something Onate didn't wish to pursue—at least for the time being

By the early 1600s, however, Spanish impact was being felt throughout the northern Sangre de Cristo Mountains. Settlers were moving in, churches were being built, and more than 2,500 Indians had, at least superficially, been converted. In 1620, a mission was established in Piwetha and, by 1650, a church and convento (priest's quarters) had been built using forced Indian labor. It appeared that at least one of Onate's goals had been fulfilled. Then came the revolt.

As part of the colonization of native lands, the Pueblo People were required to pay tribute to the Spaniards (La Encomenida) in the form of food and services. Little more than slaves, they were also forbidden to practice their own religion. By 1680, they had had enough. On August 10th, led by Luis Tupato, governor of the pueblo, the People of Piwetha joined forces with other pueblos and waged war against the Spanish soldiers, their priests, and their settlers. The local priest, Matias Rendon, was killed, the church and convento were burned to the ground, and countless numbers of Spanish citizens were massacred. The same thing happened in virtually all of the surrounding pueblos. The few remaining Spaniards fled to El Paso and many of the People of Piwetha moved to the western plains of Kansas.

In 1692, Diego de Vargas led the reconquest of New Mexico. The few remaining natives at Piwetha submitted quietly but when they saw the old Spanish regime reassert itself, they revolted again in 1696. This time, it was a losing battle and the few remaining People of Piwetha fled to the safety of their Apache friends in southern Colorado

The Apache, however, turned out to be not very good friends. They turned many of the People of Piwetha into slaves. That, coupled with the disease and epidemics sweeping the nation, greatly diminished the numbers of Piwetha People. By 1706, the remaining refugees returned to their pueblo, joined forces with the Spanish against their common foes (the Comanches and Utes), and attempted to pick up the pieces.

Life in this small, isolated village was never the same, however. Spanish settlers were encroaching on native lands, in 1746 a new church was built and dedicated to the Christian San Lorenzo (Saint Lawrence-Patron of the poor who was slowly burned to death on a gridiron), once occupied homes lay in ruins, and the population of Piwetha, now known as Picuris, had dwindled to less than 500. In 1769, raiding Comanches destroyed the new church. It wasn't rebuilt until 1776.

More recently, a new road was built connecting the Pueblo of Picuris with the outside world. In 1986, a large section of the church's wall collapsed; in 1987, the entire building was leveled and a new church, following the floor plan and exterior style of the 1770's church, was built.

Due to widespread unemployment in the area, some of the Picuris people sought employment in Santa Fe, Taos, and Los Alamos. Some of the younger people moved to the larger cities. Today, the population of the Pueblo of Picuris is less than 300.

In the spirit of their ancestors, however, it appears the People of Picuris are following their instincts and maintaining their independence. They have retained their Tribal Council and regularly elect eight members to govern the village. They have returned the bison to their land thereby providing both a food source and spiritual enhancement for their people. Pueblo members have taken the lead role in developing a regional wastewater system to protect the water for future generations. They also participate with the village of Penasco in a community coalition promoting health and wellness in the northern New Mexico villages and, in the process, celebrating life by honoring their elders through a series of oral interviews and the production of a video.

Within the pueblo, the People of Picuris are building new and improving old infrastructures to attract visitors. The Tribal Museum and Recreation Center contains historic artifacts and a small gift shop; the Hidden Valley Restaurant offers Native specialties, as well as traditional American foods; and two well-

stocked trout ponds, a picnic area, and a small campground provide the ultimate retreat for outdoor enthusiasts.

Although traditional ceremonies are still conducted in the kivas and are restricted to tribal members, other events and dances are open to the public. In late January and early February, there are various ceremonial dances. During the first weekend of July, the pueblo presents its High Country Tri-Cultural Arts & Crafts Fair and features pottery, jewelry, painting, beadwork, and weavings. The Picuris Feast Day, dedicated to the pueblo patron, San Lorenzo, is held annually on August 10th. It is usually accompanied by Vespers, morning footraces, a corn dance, a pole-climbing contest, and a sunset dance.

The pueblo is also the majority owner in a partnership that operates an up-scale hotel and Native American restaurant

in Santa Fe. Diners may even request dinner in a teepee—
something never seen on the Pueblo of Picuris.

What does the future hold for the People of the Pueblo
of Picuris? Only time will tell.

What to see:

The Pueblo of Picuris and Museum—Stop at Governor's
Office near pueblo entrance for permit to enter ruins—
Call the visitors' center about guided tours and events
schedule—505-587-2957 or 505-587-2519

San Lorenzo de Picuris Church—Not always open—Ask
at the visitors' center if locked

What to look for:

Ancient ruins
Bronze-like, mica-flecked pottery
Picuris and Pa-nu Lakes

Where to eat:

Hidden Valley Restaurant at the Pueblo Visitors' Center
Other restaurants in Penasco

Where to stay:

Call Pueblo Visitors' Center (numbers above) for
information about camping
Other accommodations in Vadito

PERSONAL NOTES:

PENASCO VALLEY

Founded:

      Penasco (Rocky Outcropping) 1796
      Vadito ((Little Ford) Around the same time
      Tres Ritos (Three Creeks) About 1900

Location:

      33-40 miles northeast of Espanola
      On State Roads 75 and 518

With the sun setting at their backs and at least another full day of travel ahead, most travelers start looking for dinner and a comfortable bed after they leave Picuris. The villages of Penasco, Vadito, and Tres Ritos, located in closed proximity to each other, offer both. But there is more than creature comforts in these adjoining towns, as any avid fisherman or skier will attest.

Laying in the shadow of the Picuris Mountains, the Rio Pueblo and Rio Santa Barbara come together at the edge of the Penasco Valley to form the Embudo Creek that flows west to join the Rio Grande near Embudo. At over nine thousand feet above sea level and flowing out of the Rio Grande Watershed, the rivers and creeks run fast and cold. Wild brown, cutthroat, and an occasional rainbow trout call these waters home but fishermen (and women) who find the best fishing holes call it Heaven. Although access to some of these spots is difficult, it's well worth the effort to find them. This may not be the best fishing in New Mexico but, after all is said and done, what's better than a good fish dinner? For those travelers that come unprepared but motivated, licenses, guides, and bait are available at any of the numerous bait shops along State Road 75, State Road 518, and at the Picuris Pueblo.

When fishing season is over, however, many outdoor aficionados pack up their fishing gear, polish up their skis and, while other families choose Santa Fe or Taos, head for Sipapu.

In the Tewa language, Sipapu can mean either a cave or cavity in the earth's surface or "Spirit Place" as it is legendary place from which the Pueblo Indians emerged. It was their point of origin. Joe Sando of Jemez Pueblo tells the story best. From his book, Pueblo Nations, he writes:

"The people came from the north to their present areas of residence, from the place of origin at Shibapu, where they emerged from the underworld by way of a lake. During their journeys, the war chief led them. This chief served for life. With his assistants and the annually appointed war captains and their staffs, he constituted a force responsible for clearing the path upon which the people traveled And with them came the Great Spirit, and He guided the ancient ones through the many arduous tasks of daily life."

Legend or fact, it seemed appropriate for Lloyd and Olive Bolander to use this ancient word to name the ski area they developed in 1952. Skiing was a fairly new phenomenon in New Mexico at the time but the Bolanders sensed that the winter sport would emerge and bring new life to the Penasco Valley. Like the war captains of old, they cleared trails and built a warming shelter and cabins. The work was difficult and demanding but, at the end of more than twenty years hard labor, the Sipapu Ski Resort included several lifts, a rental shop, restaurant, grocery store, and overnight accommodations for sixty people.

When the Bolander's son, Bruce, joined his parents in 1975, the ski area doubled in size and the lodging accommodations increased to 175. Since that time, the number of trails has increased to nineteen. They are served by three lifts: a 2900 foot triple chair, a 2800 foot Poma, and a 500 foot Poma. The trails offer a diversity of skiing from beginner's level to expert. As New Mexico Magazine writer Arnold Vigil once reported:

"Bruce now manages the resort and carries on the traditions and values of his parents—affordable skiing, comfortable accommodations, great service, and a down to earth atmosphere that can't be beat. You don't come to Sipapu to compare ski outfits or collect autographs, but there's always a roaring fire in the fireplace and a smile on the face of some friendly staff member ready to help."

If additional incentive is needed to stay in this valley overnight, consider hiking or backpacking the many trails in the nearby Carson National Forest or the Pecos Wilderness. The dense forests, green valleys, alpine lakes, rocky bluffs and outcroppings, and abundant wildlife in these remote wilderness areas provide some of the most picturesque scenery in all of northern New Mexico and help convey the fact that there is more to life than cars, jobs, stress, and anxiety.

What to see:
Nature at her finest

What to look for:
Hidden Lakes
Rocky Mountain Bighorn Sheep
Eagles
People enjoying the outdoors and all it has to offer

Where to eat:
There are a variety of places to eat in Penasco. Among them are:
Alicia's on State Road 75—505-587-1993
Victor's on State Road 75—505-587-2661
Bear Paw Pizza on State Road 75—505-587-0311

Where to stay:
Sipapu Ski and Summer Resort
On State Road 518
Vadito
505-587-2240
www.sipapunm.com

Open year around, this resort offers horseback riding, rock climbing, fishing, and golf during the warm months and snowboarding, cross-country and alpine skiing during the cold months. An arts & crafts fair is held in July and a variety of workshops, ranging from the art of fly-fishing to fabric painting, is offered. Accommodations range from roomy dormitories that sleep eight to comfy cabins for honeymoon get-aways or small families. There is also an RV Park with full hookups, except during winter months.

Tres Ritos Lodge
4920 State Road 518
Vadito
505-587-0486
www.tresritoslodge.com

If peace and quite is what you crave, Tres Ritos Lodge is the place to stay. Its comfortable cabins offer streamside decks, fireplaces, and full kitchens. But—there are no TVs or telephones—just the sounds of nature and maybe a snoring bear or two. May only be open seasonally—call ahead to be sure.

PERSONAL NOTES:

POT CREEK CULTURAL SITE

Founded:
>   Around 1130

Original name:
>   Unknown

Location:
>   40 miles east of Espanola
>   9 miles south of Taos
>   On State Road 518

Very little has been written about Pot Creek Pueblo because, to date, very little is known about its origin or the people who once lived there. However, based on scientific research, archeologists have pieced together enough data to at least offer a fragmentary glimpse into the past.

It is believed that the first people to occupy the area were Anasazi. They may have come here from Mesa Verde or Chaco Canyon as early as AD 1130 when drought and overcrowding forced some of them to relocate. These early people built scattered villages made up of shallow pithouses that had clay-lined floors, log walls packed with a mud mortar, and peeled-log roofs overlaid with juniper bark. Entrance to the pithouse was probably through a small side opening—the Anasazi were a short, stocky people and didn't need anything larger.

Hunters and gatherers, the Anasazi took whatever nature had to offer. They were a people of the earth and lived by and with it. As time progressed, they developed some agricultural skills but their tools seldom surpassed the sharp sticks they used when planting seeds. Seeds and harvests were kept in woven baskets, and later in pottery.

During the period of migration, more people came to the area, and it became necessary to build larger structures. Walls were erected over pithouses; log roofs were replaced with new floors; and ancient debris was buried or destroyed.

By the mid 1200s, multi-storied, aboveground groups of dwellings (or room blocks) covered the remains of the pithouses. Built in massive courses rather than with adobe bricks, each group of room blocks surrounded a small plaza in which a small kiva (a circular subterranean structure used for ceremonial purposes) was built. While the lower rooms of the buildings were used for storage, the upper rooms served as family quarters.

Artifacts recovered from the Site indicate that the Pot Creek inhabitants made astonishing advancements during their period of occupation. The crafts they produced included utilitarian gray cooking vessels, bone and ground stone tools, and decorated black-on-white pottery. Their crops were prospering and there was less reliance on hunting and gathering. The presence of turquoise and shell jewelry indicates they traded with other Native groups to the south and southwest. Even so, by AD 1320, the inhabitants of Pot Creek abandoned their pueblo and moved to other settlements.

Like Mesa Verde or Chaco Canyon, the reason (or reasons) for abandoning Pot Creek may never be clear. Overcrowding is one thought; another is climate. The cold winters around the Taos area might certainly have been a deterrent but Picuris, the area to which many Pot Creek residents moved, wasn't much better. So, what really happened?

Recent excavations indicate a fire may have been the cause of abandonment. According to Michael Adler, SMU Department of Anthropology: "The inside margins of the adobe walls (of several rooms) were fired orange and black, indicating an intense fire had consumed (these rooms) at sometime in the past." Samples from the burned rooms were taken over a period of two excavation seasons. "This was particularly important' states Adler 'because (the) rooms showed evidence of having been burned with artifact assemblages and stored food in place." In other words, the People didn't leave on their own accord, they were forced out.

Adolph Bandelier, self-taught in the science of archeology, was the first to report the presence of Pot Creek Pueblo (1880–1882) while touring northern New Mexico pueblos. Taking copious notes about the things he saw, he laid the foundation for future scientific explorations. But it wasn't until 1957 that active excavation and meaningful archeological research began. Since then, more than thirty-two seasons of excavation have been carried out at the Site located on the grounds of Southern Methodist University's summer campus at Fort Burgwin.

Aside from on-going excavations evident at the Cultural Site, there are reconstructions of an Anasazi dwelling and an ancient irrigation system. Visitors may tour the grounds from 9am to 4pm, Wednesday through Sunday, from late June to early September. Call 505-587-2255 (www.smu.edu/taos)for information—also ask about volunteer projects.

PERSONAL NOTES:

FORT BURGWIN

Established:
    August 14, 1852

Original name:
    Cantonment Burgwin

Location:
    40 miles east of Espanola
    9 miles south of Taos
    On State Road 518

Toward the end of the Mexican-American War, New Mexico was formally declared a U.S. Territory and, as such, protection of the Northern Frontier fell under the jurisdiction of the United States. Fort Marcy, the first U.S. military post in the Southwest, was built in Santa Fe in 1846 and in 1851 construction began on Fort Union near present-day Las Vegas. Hostile Indian attack continued to be a problem and the forts were erected to protect the frontier settlements as well as the wagon trains that brought them provisions.

Following a particularly nasty rebellion in Taos in 1847, during which Anglo settlers, public officials and Governor Charles Bent were massacred, it was decided that additional protection was needed for the villages between the two forts. The location chosen was a remote area in the valley of the Rito de la Olla (Pot Creek) along the main wagon route from Santa Fe to Taos.

Named for Captain John Burgwin who was killed in the Taos Rebellion, Cantonment Burgwin, (never officially designated a fort - cantonment is a military site classification between camp and fort) was a complex consisting of barracks, stables, kitchen, mess hall, and offices built of windowless facades and surrounding two plazas.

Life for the soldiers garrisoned at the cantonment was dismal. The encampment was miles away from any town or entertainment, the winters were long and cold, and wolves attacked the livestock. Morale was low and many men deserted. To make matters worse, military forays against the Indians proved futile. Indian attacks against the settlers continued, cattle (including those at the military post) were stolen, and the Civil War was heating up.

By 1855, Indian attacks were under control. The soldiers were bored and the buildings, no longer worth maintaining, were deteriorating. In 1860, Cantonment Burgwin was closed and the remaining troops were moved to Fort Union.

In the mid 1950s, Ralph Rounds, a lumber company owner and amateur archeologist, purchased what remained of Cantonment Burgwin. Its buildings were long gone, buried under a century of neglect and decay. With the assistance of Fred Wendorf (Professor of Anthropology at Southern Methodist University), the old encampment was resurrected, restored, and designated "Fort."

In 1964, SMU acquired the property, added student housing, a cafeteria and an auditorium. At the SMU-In-Taos Summer Campus courses in humanities, natural and social sciences, performing and studio arts are offered, and archeological and anthropological research is conducted.

From May 1 to Oct 1, visitors can walk around the campus, view restorations of the old cantonment buildings, attend lectures, musical and theatrical programs, and art shows. The Pot Creek (Rito de la Olla) Cultural Site is also located here. For further information, call 505-758-8322 in summer, or 214-768-3657 during the rest of the year. (Also see www.smu.edu/taos)

TALPA

Founded:
>   Early 1700s
>   Officially 1823

Original name:
>   Nuestra Senora del Rio Chiquito
>   Nuestra Senora de Talpa (Probably after Talpa in Jalisco, Mexico)

Location:
>   44 miles east of Espanola
>   8 miles south of Taos

After leaving Pot Creek and Fort Burgwin, most people drive through this small agricultural village without ever noticing it. The oversight is understandable because there are few signs, no roadside services, and only a handful of houses. But there is something here that makes this town worthy of a visit—its chapel.

In the early days of the Northern Frontier, villages were few and far between. Some villages had churches; others did not. Settlers in villages without churches often traveled as much as five or six miles to attend religious services at neighboring churches. In good weather, the trip was a leisurely stroll for people accustomed to traveling long distances by foot but when the snow was deep or the sun scorching it was a hardship.

The irregularity of priestly visits made matters worse. Hampered by bad weather, poor roads, and Indian attack, the priest was seldom around when needed. The every day ordeals of living in a hostile environment required daily attention and, following the tradition of their ancestors, many families created home altars.

Typically tucked into the corner of a room and adorned with dried or paper flowers, candles, and rosaries, the focal point of the home altar was the patron saint, or saints, of the family. It was believed that these saints, known as Santos, were heavenly mediators capable of granting favors such as abundant crops, good health, and well-being. Each day began and ended with prayers to the Santos; some prayers were answered, others were not.

As family size and village population increased, the need for separate buildings dedicated to the common need of community worship arose. The more prosperous citizens donated

land and funds to build capillas (chapels) used for communal
prayer services and novenas as well as for christenings and
funerals. Such was the case in Talpa.

In 1823, on land donated by Manuel Lucero, Bernardo
Duran built an adobe chapel dedicated to Nuestra Senora de
San Juan de los Lagos (Our Lady of Saint John of the Lakes).
An unassuming structure, the chapel had a single belfry and two
towers outside, wooden floors and mud-plastered walls inside.
An altar screen, painted in 1828, housed the carved image of
the patron saint as well as that of San Bernardino (Saint
Bernard), the patron of Bernardo Duran.

Although they travel to Ranchos de Taos for traditional
services, the people of Talpa still use the tiny chapel for daily
devotions and to pay homage to the Santos that have seen them
through good times and bad. They light candles and lay flowers
before the altar, they dress the Virgin in elegant gowns and jewels,
and they say simple prayers to familiar intercessors. They follow
the traditions of their ancestors and make the practice of their
faith an everyday occurrence.

Are their prayers answered? Only the faithful of Talpa
can say for sure.

What to see:
Nuestra Senora de San Juan del Rio Chiquito Chapel

What to look for:
1828 altar screen painted by Santero Molleno
Image of Our Lady of Saint John of the Lakes in center
of altar screen carved by Santero Rafael Aragon

Where to eat:
The closest restaurants are in Ranchos de Taos

Where to stay:

The closest accommodations are in Ranchos de Taos

PERSONAL NOTES:

RANCHOS DE TAOS

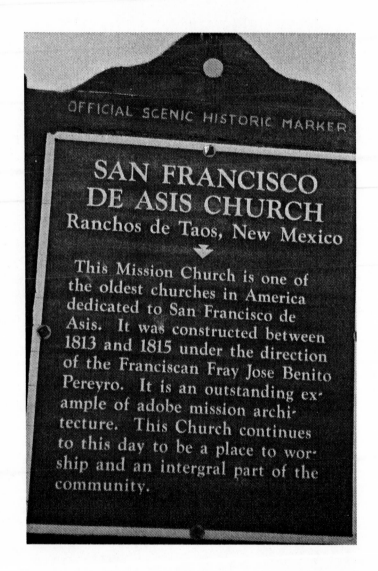

Founded:

 Originally in 1716

 Abandoned during Comanche raids in 1750s

 Resettled 1779

Original Name:

 Rio de las Trampas de Taos (River of the Traps of Taos)

 Ranchos de Don Fernando de Taos

Location:

 47 miles northeast of Espanola

 5 miles south of Taos

 At junction of State Roads 518 and 68

The year was 1779 and settlers who sought safety at the Taos Pueblo during the Comanche raids were moving back into Rio de las Trampas de Taos. In an effort to bring some degree of normalcy back to their lives, they began construction of a church—a massive adobe structure built like a fortress. Dedicated in 1815 as San Franciso de Asis (Saint Francis of Assisi), the church served as a spiritual and corporal source of sanctuary for local residents.

 In 1846, the United States invaded New Mexico, formerly under Mexican rule, declared it a new U.S. territory, and appointed Charles Bent as the new governor. All Residents were thereafter considered United States citizens, an aspect acceptable to the Anglos but not to the Hispanos or Natives who were fearful the new government would strip them of their rights and lands. In a plot to regain New Mexico for Mexico, a band of Taos rebels enlisted the aid of the Taos Pueblo Indians, attacked the Anglo village of Taos, killed many of the settlers, most of the officials, and the governor.

During the fracas, people hid in the almost windowless church and prayed for safety. God must have heard their prayers because, although the church at the Taos Pueblo was destroyed during the battle, San Francisco de Asis came through unharmed.

The walls of the church are four feet thick and buttresses, both front and back, measure as much as ten feet in places. Not counting the walls, the church measures 108 feet in length and

35 feet in width. Beams and vigas imbedded in the walls support the ceiling of the two-story interior.

The exterior walls of the church are mud-plastered. Due to the extreme climate of this region, every square inch of the surface is renewed annually during a weeklong community project in which young and old participate. They mix sand, water, and straw; use sheepskins to apply the mixture to the walls; carry buckets; serve food; and do whatever it takes to get the job done. Needless to say, everyone enjoys the task and all who see the church admire their efforts. In fact, San Francisco de Asis Church is noted as being the most photographed church in New Mexico.

The interior of the church contains a French-style altar as well as the work of early Santeros. Bultos, retablos, and reredos line the walls. There is also a large cedar carving of Saint Francis of Assissi, the patron of the church. But one of the most striking features is a painting, not in the church but in a building adjacent to it.

Created in 1896 by the French-Canadian artist Henri Ault, the painting depicts Jesus Christ standing on a rock surrounded by water. His left hand hangs at his side and His right hand rests over His heart. Named The Shadow of the Cross, there is nothing unusual about this painting...until the lights are turned off. Then, as viewers' eyes become accustomed to the dark, something miraculous happens: the entire background of the painting begins to glow and the figure of Christ appears as if in silhouette with a halo above His head and the shadow of the Cross at His back. Once the lights are turned back on, the painting returns to normal.

This phenomenon was first witnessed by the artist when he returned to his studio one night after completing the painting. A strange glow lit up the room as he entered the otherwise darkened studio. At first, he thought he might have left a fire burning, but then he realized the glow was coming from the painting. Upon closer inspection, he saw the halo and cross, neither of which he painted into the picture. How could this be?

Word of the mysterious painting made its way around the world. In 1904, it was exhibited at the St. Louis World's Fair and later it was taken on a tour of Europe. Scientists examined the painting, trying to find an explanation. The paints Ault used were tested, chemicals were applied to the painting, and Geiger counters were employed. The results were always the same—there was no scientific explanation.

In 1948, Mrs. Herbert Sydney Griffin of Wichita Falls, Texas purchased the painting. Mrs. Griffin believed the painting had been created by the hand of God and, as such, rightfully belonged in a church. The church she chose was San Francisco de Asis in Ranchos de Taos, a place of peace, a place of sanctuary, a place of renewal.

Do miracles happen? The fact that this church survived Indian attacks, a major rebellion, and the onslaught of time seems to prove they do. However, judging by the number of parishioners who regularly attend services here, it seems the real miracle is the deep devotion and determination of the people who, regardless of what happens around them, carry out the traditions of their ancestors and preserve a heritage that is meaningful, relevant, and of great importance.

What to see:

San Franciso de Asis Mission Church—Open Monday thru Saturday 9am to 4pm
The Shadow of the Cross Painting—Donation required—Last showing 3pm Monday thru Saturday
Ranchos de Taos Plaza around the church—Unique shops and galleries

What to look for:

Santos, tinwork, woodcarving, miracles

Photo opportunities—Best in early morning or late afternoon

Where to eat:

Joseph's Table

Highway 68 one block north of San Francisco de Asis Church

Open for lunch and dinner (call for hours)

505-751-4512

The Taos Art Colony seems to have spilled over into this one room restaurant. It's a fun place, with birdcages hanging from the ceiling and candles lighting up water-splashed walls. And the food—everything from exotic Chilean sea bass to down home bread pudding. The perfect ending to the perfect day.

Ranchos Plaza Grill

Open for breakfast, lunch, and dinner

On the plaza surrounding San Francisco de Asis Church

505-758-8100

An authentic 200 year old adobe hacienda next to the church, serving Native New Mexican cuisine and international delights.

Additional restaurants located in Taos

Adobe & Pines Inn
On State Road 68 one block south of San Francisco de
Asis
505-751-0947
www.adobepines.com

Centered around an 1830s adobe hacienda and
surrounded by two-and-a- half acres of gardens, fruit trees,
cottonwoods, blue spruce, and willow, this inn offers
private decks for stargazing, fireplaces for warming up,
and jetted tubs for relaxing. Southwestern furnishings
reflect the warmth and serenity of the surrounding
countryside. And, in the morning, a gourmet breakfast
is served in a room overlooking a flower-filled courtyard.

Additional accommodations available in Taos

PERSONAL NOTES:

MORE INFORMATION

Now that you've completed your armchair journey Along the High Road, you might find the following books interesting:

GENERAL HISTORY

Fugate, Francis L. and Roberta B. *Roadside History of New Mexico.* Mountain Press Publishing, Missoula. 1989.

Jenkins, Mary Ellen and Albert H. Schroeder. *A Brief History of New Mexico.* University of New Mexico Press, Albuquerque. 1974.

Julyan, Robert. *The Place Names of New Mexico.* University of New Mexico Press, Albuquerque. 1996.

Noble, David Grant. *Pueblos, Villages, Forts and Trails.* University of New Mexico Press, Albuquerque. 1994.

Simmons, Marc. *New Mexico: An Interpretive History.* University of New Mexico Press, Albuquerque. 1998.

GENERAL ARTS

Cirillo, Dexter. *Across Frontiers: Hispanic Crafts of New Mexico.* Chronicle Books, San Francisco. 1998.

Spanish Colonial Arts Society. *Hispanic Arts and Ethnohistory in the Southwest.* Ancient City Press, Santa Fe. 1993.

ARCHEOLOGICAL AND NATIVE HISTORY

Fontana, Bernard L. *A Guide to Contemporary Southwest Indians.* Southwest Parks and Monuments Association, Tucson. 1999.

Lister, Robert H. and Florence C. *Those Who Came Before.* University of New Mexico Press, Albuquerque. 1994.

Mays, Buddy. *Indian Villages of the Southwest.* Chronicle Books, San Francisco. 1985.

CHURCHES

Cash, Marie Romero. *Built of Earth and Song.* Red Crane Books, Santa Fe. 1993.Prince,

L. Bradford. *Spanish Mission Churches of New Mexico.* Rio Grande Press, Glorieta. 1977.

CULTURE

Coles, Robert. *The Old Ones of New Mexico.* University of New Mexico Press, Albuquerque. 1973

Crutchfield, James A. *It Happened in New Mexico.* Falcon Publishing, Helena. 1995.

Kay, Elizabeth. *Chimayo Valley Traditions.* Ancient City Press, Santa Fe. 1987

SANTOS AND SANTEROS

Boyd, E. *Saint & Saint Makers* (Revised). Western Edge Press, Santa Fe. 1998.

Giffords, Gloria Fraser. *Mexican Folk Retablos* (Revised). University of New Mexico Press, Albuquerque. 1974.

Martinez, Eluid Levi. *What is a New Mexico Santo?* (Revised). Sunstone Press, Santa Fe. 1992

Steele, Thomas J. *Santos and Saints*. Ancient City Press, Santa Fe. 1974

PENITENTES

Chavez, Fray Angelico. *My Penitente Land*. Museum of New Mexico Press, Santa Fe. 1974

Horka-Follick, Lorayne Ann. *Los Hermanos Penitentes*. Westernlore Press, Los Angeles. 1969

Pulido, Alberto Lopez. *The Sacred World of the Penitentes*. Smithsonian Institution Press, Washington and London. 2000.

Weigle, Marta. *The Penitentes of the Southwest*. Ancient City Press, Santa Fe. 1970.

Wroth, William. *Images of Penance, Images of Mercy*. University of Oklahoma Press, Norman. 1991.

To view examples of the arts, cultures, and life-styles of Northern
Frontier settlers, please visit the following:

Museum of International Folk Art
706 Camino Lejo
Santa Fe
505-827-6350
www.nmoca.org

Museum of Spanish Colonial Art
750 Camino Lejo
Santa Fe
505-982-2226
www.spanishcolonial.org

Albuquerque Museum
2000 Mountain Road NW
Albuquerque
505-243-7255
www.cabq.gov/museum

National Hispanic Cultural Center of New Mexico
1701 4th Street SW
Albuquerque
505-246-2261
www.nhccnm.org

Indian Pueblo Cultural Center
2401 12th Street NW
Albuquerque
800-766-4405
505-843-7270
www.indianpueblo.org

Cristo Rey Church
Upper Canyon Road
Santa Fe
505-983-8528

St. Francis Cathedral
Cathedral Place at San Francisco Street
Santa Fe
505-982-5619

Casa San Ysidro (closed in December & January)
Old Church Road
Corrales
Call Dee Turner–505-898-3915 or
Albuquerque Museum–505-243-7255

El Rancho de las Golondrinas (Open April through October)
334 Los Pinos Road
La Cieniga
505-471-2261
www.golondrinas.org